PENGUIN B(

MUSEUM OF THE AMERICAS

Selected for the National Poetry Series in 2017 and a recipient of the Walt Whitman Award from the Academy of American Poets, J. Michael Martinez is the author of three collections of poetry. He is a poetry editor of Noemi Press, a CantoMundo Fellow, and his writings have been anthologized in Ahsahta Press's *The Arcadia Project: North American Postmodern Pastoral,* Rescue Press's *The New Census: An Anthology of Contemporary American Poetry,* and Counterpath Press's *Angels of the Americlypse: New Latin@ Writing.* Visiting assistant professor of poetry at St. Lawrence University, J. Michael lives in upstate New York.

THE NATIONAL POETRY SERIES

The National Poetry Series was established in 1978 to ensure the publication of five collections of poetry annually through five participating publishers. The Series is funded annually by Amazon Literary Partnership, Betsy Community Fund, the Gettinger Family Foundation, Bruce Gibney, HarperCollins Publishers, Stephen King, Lannan Foundation, Newman's Own Foundation, News Corp, Anna and Olafur Olafsson, the O. R. Foundation, the PG Family Foundation, the Poetry Foundation, Laura and Robert Sillerman, Amy R. Tan and Louis De Mattei, Elise and Steven Trulaske, and the National Poetry Series Board of Directors.

• 2017 COMPETITION WINNERS •

The Lumberjack's Dove
by GennaRose Nethercott,
chosen by Louise Gluck for Ecco

Anarcha Speaks
by Dominique Christina,
chosen by Tyehimba Jess for Beacon Press

feeld
by Jos Charles,
chosen by Fady Joudah for Milkweed Editions

What It Doesn't Have to Do With
by Lindsay Bernal,
chosen by Paul Guest for University of Georgia Press

Museum of the Americas
by J. Michael Martinez,
chosen by Cornelius Eady for Penguin Books

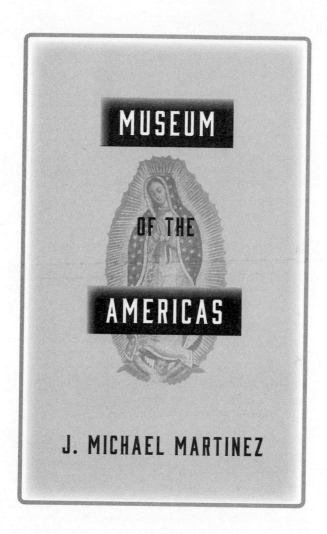

MUSEUM

OF THE

AMERICAS

J. MICHAEL MARTINEZ

PENGUIN BOOKS

PENGUIN BOOKS

An imprint of Penguin Random House LLC
375 Hudson Street
New York, New York 10014
penguinrandomhouse.com

Page 1: Courtesy of the author
Page 21: Getty Research Institute, Los Angeles (89.R.46)
Page 33: Courtesy of *The State Journal-Register*
Page 91: Courtesy of the author

Acknowledgments to the original publishers
of the poems in this book appear on page 87.

LIBRARY OF CONGRESS CATALOGING-IN-PUBLICATION DATA
Names: Martinez, J. Michael, 1978– author.
Title: Museum of the Americas / J. Michael Martinez.
Description: New York, New York : Penguin Books, 2018. | Series:
National poetry series
Identifiers: LCCN 2018015372 (print) | LCCN 2018018181 (ebook) |
ISBN 9780525505235 (Ebook) | ISBN 9780143133445 (paperback)
Subjects: | BISAC: POETRY / American / General. | POETRY / American /
Hispanic American.
Classification: LCC PS3613.A78644 (ebook) | LCC PS3613.A78644 A6 2018 (print) |
DDC 811/.6—dc23
LC record available at https://lccn.loc.gov/2018015372

Printed in the United States of America

3   5   7   9   10   8   6   4   2

Set in Bembo Std
Designed by Elyse J. Strongin, Neuwirth & Associates

in memory of M.J.M.
&, always, for Swift

In allegory the observer is confronted with the *facies hippocratica* of history as a petrified, primordial landscape. Everything about history that, from the very beginning, has been untimely, sorrowful, unsuccessful, is expressed in a face—or rather in a death's head. And although such a thing lacks all "symbolic" freedom of expression, all classical proportion, all humanity— nevertheless, this is the form in which man's subjection to nature is most obvious and it significantly gives rise not only to the enigmatic question of the nature of human existence as such, but also of the biographical historicity of the individual.

This is the heart of the allegorical way of seeing.

—WALTER BENJAMIN

CONTENTS

I

II

III

IV

MUSEUM OF THE AMERICAS

I

JERRY MARTINEZ & MARY MARTINEZ, 1974

The body becomes an effect of the language that seeks to describe it.

—ERIN GOSS, *Revealing Bodies*

POTUS XLV

this pivot
point so carcass

carved: servant who sweetens
only mirrors, where is
the milk?

CROSSING THE BORDER
Laredo, Texas

Where we were [   ]
[   ] lilac lisianthus

Where what has been written
must be [   ]

[   ] sands [   ] once fertile [   ],
droughts [   ] once flood

Where yellowed leaves [   ]
[   ] the river, [   ] of lilacs

Where within [   ]
[   ]
human law, our fluent dependencies.

Where the water [   ] strains
[   ] long for [   ]

[   ] this Garden,
[   ] of distance

relinquishing self to [   ],
harbor [   ].

Now, without, I echo
[   ] edge, [   ],

sowing [   ]
& flesh [   ]

[   ] bodies [   ]
[   ] in each other's secrets,

[   ] web [   ]
[   ] the mouth of birds.

INSTRUCTIONS FOR IDENTIFYING "ILLEGAL" IMMIGRANTS

i.   Consider moving through
the preface to *home*:

> the crowns
> & field stones
>
> littered.

ii.   Consider skin's nature
departure's hue:

> the immigrant will be
> dried leaves amongst owl eggs
>
> & cradles
> of lacquered oak.

iii.   Recall you are homeland
& formal choice

> coiled in accent around
> a room whose edges dream themselves
> into shapelessness.

iv.   Consider the white
body as passport,

> the flesh the barrier
> of no specific light
>
>
> held where every edge is erosion,
> endings open
>
> into endless nudity.

TREATY OF GUADALUPE HIDALGO

A candle: presented in the water

Shall the boundary: seen before the boundary: lift the law:

To the end as may be: to the end as first the fountain of a lower key: the
guaranty the virtue behind clarity which I make you: for this where

      neither dove nor crow has flown:

As the *now* to ascertain, in the *yet* obscured: we speak juxtaposed: in the
juxtaposed: without knowing what wills the ruins:

This treaty shall be: this treaty shall be: the boundary seen before the
signature: we speak now: the fountain of a lower key: the guaranty: the
greater wilt the virtue behind

      clarity: with bells on his ankles in the margins of story:

The treaty of amity, commerce & navigation: the treatise to fortify: in the
name of you: through virtue: in the near as you: the wilt which is body: a
candle in water

With the *now* to ascertain, with it ever yet: shall the boundary be the
boundary not the treaty: we speak the *yet*: a single candle: where the
content exceeds the phrase:

We speak the candle: we speak water to announce the end:
to sincerity's calamities: desire the end as may be:

      with it every yet, as the snow is to ascertain in it:
      near as you: the ruins where the will is free.

ROSARY (PRAYER ONE)

Wherein she martyrs the mirror:
      this carnival of stone,
      her lips dilate
      the negation—space into starpoint

Wherein she, to be both sacrum & wrist—
      neither the fugitive epidermis,
      nor the unlocked ashblack—
      sovereigns the shadow swell as love

Wherein she ardors the emptiness open,
      proof the unanchored
      Spirit of my silence,
      her revisions clothing my brightest orgasm—

Wherein she says, I can hear you,
      the seed under the belly's flesh—love the far shore,

      she says, For *She* withdraws the Spring wild.

FAMILY PHOTO—MI BISABUELA CON MI ABUELA

Maria Beltran would peel the oranges
& all things on the earth's surface
became navel & hearth

She balances Maria Jesus
where becoming takes the form
of the process of weaving

the baby's cap, frilled gray,
awash in a single energy,
spirals a small face a white gold

& the child's fingers cling
within the unfolding reality,
about to fall, balanced on the bench,

by her mother's arm steadying
each interwoven constellation
cascading to flowers

LORD, SPANGLISH ME

i.

Lord, Spanglish mi abuela para mi

>boil the orange rind
>beneath the syntax
>peeled of her name

>translate *naranja*   into *familia*
>the grove   into tea,
>the tea   into the talisman

>of her hand's soft work,
>the color of fold,

>unfolded,
>>& sung.

ii.

Lord, Spanglish mi abuela para mi

>her kingdom creation come,
>her gray hair grown down the fears,

>her pale hand plucking
>my tears as plums
>as love ransoms

>the noun within,
>her childhood unseeded

>>beneath the ravage,
>the creek drowning

>her colony home,
>the aphids   & the oak,

>her velvet Christ flood-spent,
>>& Godless.

iii.

Lord, Spanglish mi madre para ti

> carve shipless the light
> my world is etched by
> the wreck-salt
> so she may move
> among the beryl water,
> tide red with the silt
> beneath baptism, her eyes cast
> in the shadow of the soft
> of lavender grown there.

iv.

Lord, Spanglish mi lengua para ti

> that I may break open
> the promise-space of my fear,
> & become ladder, &

I may finally skin my ravage,

> that I may bear the estranged seasons,
> for I know we are creatures of metal
> without answer,

> a lost Spring
> whose lips rest
> where intimacy resigned
>   the shapes of want,

> our honey succored from dust.

FAMILY PHOTO—SLICING THEIR WEDDING CAKE

They were the story time
& she, the elven smile

wearing a dove falling to frosting
& the curtains amber the parturient

father shape blurred inside
the foreground, auburn bright in snowed

shirt ruffles, his eyes eyelash thin
ravens & the lantern warmth

of peach fur brightens
& her wedding dress spills

lilies & lilies of sugar mornings

CASTA PAINTINGS, AN EROTICS OF NEGATION

> I know something about race and about sex and I obey
> the market imperative
> to keep things moving.

> —Farid Matuk, "History as a War of Poses"

◉

Over her honey-hued skin the woman wears a blue ruffled dress & stands beside the pale man; stitched flowers vine up & down her apron. He sports a gold-buttoned black uniform, white stockings reach to his knees. At a distance, an "Indian" woman carries a basket of corn; the man beside her in a sarape holds a bag of squash; their child, between them, gazes up

beyond both mother & father.

Of such fertile I's,
this Gold discerns

a portrait wrapped
the worlds through us.

Divided by thin black lines, the foreground & subjects ornately dominate one's attention: the indistinct beige background contrasts sharply with these garish depictions.

◉

The calligraphic script underscoring each panel *doesn't* name these figures
with specific proper nouns; rather, the calligraphy titles each figure a
representative of a general racial species; these people are not individuals
but specimens: this man designates *the* "Spanish," the woman is *the*
"mulatta," and their child, carrying a basket of fruit, *Nace torna atras*,
"a Return-backwards is Born." Language & oil combine to boundary
the body into "race." Ideologically or conceptually activated upon the
represented body through the oddly poetic proper noun, "race," at times,
manifests not as nouns, but verbs ostensibly held in stasis: *Nace torna atras*,
"a Return-backwards is Born," or *Salta atras, sale tente en el aire*, "a Return-
backwards Makes Hold-Yourself-Suspended-in-Midair."

In the 18th & into the 19th century, casta paintings were employed in New Spain to validate racial identity ("whiteness") in the legislation of land acquisition & in determining civil rights.

Engaged upon the background's horizonless beige, the figures appear as forms outside the social, standing as racial indices prior to particularities.

The castas were portrayals of a single individual's heredity: canvas brushed with numerous tiled panels

        depicting diverse domestic

                scenes, flowers & sieved selves
                  gathered for gold.

The background's beige as the ruptured space-time of the confessional: the sixteen panels, while of distinct portraits, are nevertheless united on one canvas; in point of fact, its social purpose was to portray & confess the diverse racial heredity of a single individual.

As the body is networked & united through its nervous & perceptual systems to the ecological networks of the physical world, the black lines framing each panel act as the casta's peripheral nervous system: an arrangement of black fibers branching through & linking each of the image's temporal occasions, extending outward to aesthetic, juridical & economic structures.

> Black-veined, she bursts: corporeal
> motif coppered between
>
> the name
> & sight.

While the panels depict heterosexual couples with offspring, the particular individual whose overall genetic heredity is portrayed, unknowingly, reveals a wonderfully perverse range of sexual cravings:

> the desire of man for
> man of the desire
> of woman for man of man
> of woman for the desire of woman
> for the child for father, for mother of woman
> for the call listening for the Nothing-answer
>
>   & its sweet bouquet
>   opening

Implicit to the "white" gaze demanding the creation of the casta: the desire to visually represent ancestors & their sexual relations for public consumption & legal proof.

    The cast: kinky historiographical exhibitionism. Sextastic.

all aware locked
      under this casting
      even steel may be

soft as rosefelt–
      wine, clot-stars
      held up

the thesis ALL
      demands exile
      from the stem

analogous there–
      in, I
      am practiced

Stranded in the beige, the woman & child are verbs caught in stasis by
the compound noun, waiting without realizing they are the very life
whose arrival they one day expect.

She stares into the distance as her naked child ever labors under a
basket of avocados. In the panel above, finger uncoiling in accusation,
a "white" woman directs the "Indian" cook on how to hold a spoon. At
the canvas base, a child dances in a wheat field beside his "negro" father.
The beige horizon exposes all bodies to splinters of names.

The castas: a litheness of flesh

flush in lisianthus, where miscegenation could be

articulated
&, potentially,

purified vis-à-vis the canvas.

And the canvas asked, "What was the sound the blood sang when found?
How are bodies opened like lotus under the white

motion of night?"

I enter the
frame
& point

at each other,
"I *this* I *this*,
will be *this*;

here, now, *we*
are the *I*
within *you*,"

a Narcissus
of purer erasure.

II

Horne, Walter H., Execution in Mexico, ca. 1911–1916.

[The photograph] is still a space to reorganize our thoughts about reality and our place in the world.

How do you disentangle the surface of reality?

—GILLES PERESS,
in Susie Linfield, *The Cruel Radiance: Photography and Political Violence*

Photographs of trauma present to the viewer representations that call into question the habitual reliance on vision as the principal ground for cognition. Each photograph, by virtue of the medium, inevitably turns the viewer into a latecomer at the depicted site. It thus summons him or her to a kind of vigilant and responsible viewing that will not foreclose the potential for understanding the full range of human experience—what Bataille terms "the totality of *what is.*"

—ULRICH BAER,
Spectral Evidence: The Photography of Trauma

THE MEXICAN WAR PHOTO POSTCARD COMPANY

On March 9th, 1916, General Francisco "Pancho" Villa raided the village of Columbus, New Mexico. The townspeople were executed with soldiers of the 13th U.S. Cavalry. The town, pillaged & burned.

A few days after, Walter H. Horne of *The Mexican War Photo Postcard Company* documented a village possessed by ruin:

> the images are a phantasmagoria
> of smoldering stone, of smoke
>
> curdling over cremation
> pits of Villista revolutionaries,
>
> & snapshots of the dilated
> eyes of roan stallions.

Employing an inexpensive emulsion called "gaslight," Horne printed tens of thousands of postcards. Selling thousands of his "real-photo" cards to U.S. soldiers during the Mexican Revolution, Horne was responsible for a vast photographic immigration

> of nameless Mexicans desired only as epistles
>
> anchored in their death;
> the dialectic between Self
>
> as Subject & Self
>
> as Object separated by panes of clarity
> into softer yellows.

"TRIPLE EXECUTION IN MEXICO"
A Postcard Set by Walter H. Horne

i.

White frames the sepia

       & six rifles raise
       as gateways respiring

             linguistic traces;

ever of his death, the executed
shuffles over exodus

       as if dancing:

       fingers cawed in black, chin

obscure against the tumor'd

pearls of smoke,   body as text now one

          of those things the shadow outlines
          on which is built another chariot.

ii.

Unnailed in cross,   the second
leans forward into crucifixion

arms upstretched as wingbones
wrought of tar. Quickened as postcard,

he would be drowned
in sodium carbonate:

brown bowl haircut & coveralls,
grimacing & eyes pitched

in clouds of silver halide.
Smoke rises in minor triumph

behind him as if the soul
were the emulsion

evading the image.
Lined as background stick figures,

a crowd of children gathers dust
& shade beside the spectacle:

if there are tears, there are no homilies;
if there is color, they are bronze;

if there is life, it is public domain;
if he had a name, it is now transnational

            confusion
            postmarked in relief.

iii.

Face a soft blur beneath his hair, the boy leans stiffly as if posing against
the palisade. Hide boots are scuffed gray with dirt. A book peeks up from
his jacket pocket. The words weigh the pocket down. He leans. A young
riot, his hair parts into a black gorge against his cheek. Handwritten, he
is titled, "Triple Execution in Mexico #3." Handwritten, the book peeks
forward as if to part from his falling. His hand raises as if for an offered
kiss. The left hand looses a coin. The coin falls into his title. The title is
drawn where even shape hesitates. To his left, the two words he will join
stare thru the paper sky.

"BODIES OF 3 MEN LYING AS THEY FELL AFTER BEING EXECUTED"
A Postcard by Walter H. Horne

We are
a thousand
petals to no

one

"EXECUTION IN MEXICO"
A Postcard by Walter H. Horne

Composed for the golden ratio, the boys hang from the mesquite. They
know nothing of adolescence. Facing each other, their bodies blur into
landscape—the older boy's head rests to the side as if listening for a
whisper; noose taut, his left hand raised, cradling a brighter spill to his
chest. The younger boy's chin is lost up in leaf shadow, rope crushing his
neck to the branch.

However, they are shoeless &, to the far right, three men in linen suits fade
white as smiles
     into the background.

They are shoeless &, above them, the branches tangle for a crown of
bronze light ever
     arriving & still.

     Perpetually of this acetate death, they are always in each other's hand.

"YNCINERACION DE CADAVERES EN BALBUENA"
Postcard No. 35

The mound of piled cadavers
        splays in clots of coal
        coated skin;

faces clamor
        & throb as one

hundred arms, stiff as singed tin
        soldiers,

reach across this drowning
        as if casting their names
        between the surface & depth

        of the postcard's visual space.
        Nearly lost to the border,

            an iron bed
frame, weighted black   by crumbling mouths,
        performs its last purpose in solitude.

        &, centered below their title, smoke rises

        like a flag from the ragged

        clothing   burnt to calcium

          white: violence seizing

        the emblem   as flesh
          collapses through fact.

"ONE GRAVE FOR 63 MEN AFTER THE BIG BATTLE"
A Postcard by Walter H. Horne

Rectangular,   the resting
          place:
                  a canal
                  & shoveled sand

      streak the amber heap

           of soft
         colloid corpses.

In parallel rows
        men shovel
        the soil, faceless
        bodies bent,

        all spirit
        labor obscured.

     In the background,
     centered on the horizon line,

     a woman is a black steeple beside a carriage.

At the foot of the postcard, a boy's bare torso

     arches back as if to take
     the starkest breath   between the title
                    & the copyright,

     head turning away   back & to the left
                    as two thin tears
        in the paper
        spill down
                    his cheek to his ear.

"EXECUTING BANDITS IN MEXICO"
A Postcard by Walter H. Horne

Blindfolded before the creosote,
the man waits. Out of the pale,

embodied thru copper contrast,

the executioners anchor the foreground:
six rifles raise toward the subject

line, cacti faint against the border.

The man's arms are
amputated by luminance,

as his boots crush the gray pickleweed.

A single tentacle sky
blanches the background,

absence throttling
the aperture light.

"THE EXECUTIONER'S PALISADE"
A Postcard by Walter H. Horne

One wall binds
death to death,

a partition of skin,
adrenaline & hair.

Adobe
& mesquite

pull bodies without flesh northward,
migrant anatomy ever unlocked

as the otherside of language.
Stamped for address,

the paper carcass seals
                word to image,
                postscript to passage;

the Mexican—all virgin talisman
when mailed in a sepia ruin

whose only wound is postage—
the distance the body travels
        to know another.

Yet, they, dark gardens, swing exhausted,
rebroken & rewritten

into simpler stems, leaves, & seeds,
body laid between

                what only flesh can mediate
                while flesh.

III

For a collector—and I mean a real collector, a collector as he ought to be—ownership is the most intimate relationship that one can have to objects. Not that they come alive in him; it is he who lives in them.

—WALTER BENJAMIN

Rather than embodying an alien and coercive principle of power which aimed to cow the people into submission, the museum—addressing the people as a public, as citizens—aimed to inveigle the general populace into complicity with power by placing them on this side of a power which it represented to it as its own.

—TONY BENNETT,
The Birth of the Museum: History, Theory, Politics

THE HEAD OF JOAQUIN MURRIETA

Yo soy Joaquín
perdido en un mundo de confusión

—Rodolfo "Corky" Gonzales

Touring the state of California in 1853, the "criminal" Joaquin Murrieta's decapitated and pickled head was described as "that of a man about the middle size . . . the mouth indicative at once of sensuality, cruelty & firmness. . . . The eyes, now closed in death, are said to have been dark blue, with a keen restless glance & when excited a glare of ferocity like that of an infuriated tiger. . . . The death of this monster is an occasion for general rejoicing."

In simile, his lifeless head became indicative of uncontainable animality. The macabre exhibition of the man's head *is* of a proud hunter presenting the trophy of a successful hunt. In this spectacle, Murrieta's decapitated head is

more allegory than epidermis,

echoing outside:

toward image,

the grave

obfuscating sovereignty

◎

In 1836, just outside Mexico City, General Antonio López de Santa Anna
officiated an unwarranted state funeral: contained in a crystal jar encircled
by flowers & state officials, General Santa Anna interred his amputated leg
beneath a monument.

Reported throughout Mexico & the United States, the odd spectacle
rendered the General's partial loss as total; made "real" vis-à-vis ritual
synecdoche, an imperfect sacrifice became

      absolute sacrifice   where semblance breathes

             the ash we will

             enter on our turning.

◎

In June 1847, P. T. Barnum opened the American Museum in New York City on the corner of Broadway & Ann Street. Among its oddities was the prosthetic leg of General Antonio López de Santa Anna. Shortly after the museum's opening, Herman Melville reported on the prosthetic in his contributions to the newspaper *Yankee Doodle*. Melville wrote, "We give an interior view of the Barnum Property, embracing a life-sized exhibition of the great Santa-Anna Boot, which has been brought on—by the loops by two able-bodied young Negroes—direct from the seat of war." Even for Melville, the "negro" bodies were an additional commodity of parts for exhibition.

Since Barnum's exhibit, the prosthesis has been held, from 1922 to the present day, at the Illinois State Military Museum. The Illinois sergeant who originally stole the wood & cork prosthesis was recorded as having shown the leg at county fairs & festivals for "a dime a peek."

According to rumor, the prosthesis was acquired during an ambush when the General, who had been lunching on roast chicken, fled on one leg. Stolen & interred as an exhibit in a museum of American history, the prosthesis is itself an exhibition of the relationship between the Mexican body, the political, & the aesthetic. It is an art object connoting both imperial agency & empire.

The prosthesis: where the migrant body—both the fleshed & the fashioned (a leg of wood & cork), homeless & foreign to itself—gains political currency only insofar as it is also a nationally unanchored art object, colors divorced from sight.

Articles VIII & IX of the Treaty of Guadalupe Hidalgo, ratified in 1848 by the Mexican & U.S. governments, negotiates the political citizenship & national identifications of those Mexicans living within the land ceded to the U.S. at the end of the U.S.-Mexican War.

Article VIII adjudicates, concerning those who have not yet selected either Mexican or U.S. citizenship, that "after the expiration of that year, without having declared their intention to retain the character of Mexicans, *shall be considered to have elected to become* citizens of the United States" (italics my own).

Article IX ambiguates, these peoples "shall be incorporated into the Union of the United States & be admitted, at the proper time (to be judged of by the Congress of the United States) . . ." The wording of the two articles arbitrates a fluid & unsettled space of identification.

Article VIII details how those peoples who have not made a formal declaration to return to Mexico or "to become" citizens of the U.S. are incorporated into an inconclusive space: non-action was interpreted as an implicit intention to retain the "character" of Mexicans; however, this is joined with the legislative decision to designate them, not citizens of the U.S., but as having elected *to initiate the process of becoming* citizens.

Neither this, nor that, these peoples were a method of wind, dispossessed of their former national self at the beginning of a becoming. As such, they became bodies possessed & haunted by an aesthetic committed to vanishing, the world's light opened in a hollow finger.

General Santa Anna's prosthetic leans coquettishly against its glass case. Iron coils, wine-spotted with age, sprout just above the knee. Knotted sweetly in a bow, leather cords dangle from the metal. The prosthetic leg is, after a century & a half, a sickly amber hue. Cracked & splintered, it is as if the historical were a slow eruption rising from within the artful prosthesis.

Where before I gathered flesh for the Gardener
Where before I was shelter for gestures of laurel

Where before I brimmed with separate vertebrae
Where before a shadow exhausted of air printed *life*
        onto the eminence allowing inspiration

Where before the woman's habit, the issuing of blood
Where before the cage colored with birth-fire, gnawed streams

Where before the child, heart & seasons inexhaustible
Where before the flesh veiled still in sense, execution

Where before the hand without blood took & seeded
Where before the hand seeded & sang new flesh

"Elected to become" cultivates an ontic political vacuum where the soul is excluded

& the mouth opens
as the only portal

heaven will acknowledge.

According to Article IX,

> only U.S. Congress could arbitrate this process of becoming "*at the proper time*." National identity became bodiless longing, strung into a hollow echo of *wait*, where before the hand seeded & sang new flesh, now, the "I" brimmed with separate vertebrae, beginning touch exhausted of air.
>
> Legislated into a state of citizenship turned ontological vacuum, individuals caught in this cycle of aesthetic framing of identity were hollowed into sphered mirrors

> > of a wormhole. A silver tear
> > in a shower of a thousand tears
> > in no-space falling

> > (each the space of preparation
> > before & between
> > absence & presence,

> > each what passes
> > as presence
> > passes to absence,

    what is

        the preparer
        & the space & tools
        of preparation).

Richard Griswold del Castillo, in his *The Treaty of Guadalupe Hidalgo: A Legacy of Conflict*, resolves, "In the first half century after ratification of the Treaty of Guadalupe Hidalgo, hundreds of state, territorial, & federal legal bodies produced a complex tapestry of conflicting opinions & decisions." This tapestry of opinions & decisions were, more often than not, woven from the federal court's racialization *projected onto* the unmoored.

As Dr. Martha Menchaca states in her analysis of racialization at this time, "This move had a severe impact on Mexicans because the state legislators chose not to give most people of color the legal rights enjoyed by White citizens."

If one was of "color," one was left nationally unanchored, a noun noosed animal placeless in the marrow; if one was legally rendered "white," one might enjoy civil rights, axe crowned & bonded for dawn.

The casta paintings, General Santa Anna's prosthetic leg, & Walter Horne's morbid postcards make transparent where the deep root of the noun gathers: an oval room in beginning, light broken over bare girding, every edge an erosion rawed by kingdom.

The plenitude of racial identities revealed by the casta paintings exposes these unanchored forms: in the case of General Santa Anna, the *perceived* racial body is revealed as a prosthesis, an art object of imperial fashioning. So too, the Treaty of Guadalupe may be seen as not only a political treaty between countries, but as a kind of fashioned poetic of ever emergent subjectivities. Legislated without boundary, these peoples became foreign unto themselves, poltergeists of a former flesh. Neither this nor that but as visions of corporeality, in time, each traverses historical vanishing, an archive of colored flesh, naked of nation.

The Treaty of Guadalupe: a poetic where the historical subject traverses through vanishing into the *naked color* identical in time to its embodied "self."

Like a rotten melon, this existential contradiction cracks open under its own weight, exposing a wretched excess:

unmooring flesh into index

each an archetype for the other

both ontologically & ontically,

aesthetically & in legislative realities,

in the field of ontic plenitude,

the lamenting historical self exceeds becoming—pluralizing subjectivities,

the "I" activated

as a "we" shape

preparing time:

face sieved through silk,   body's silhouette loosened

from body's flute,

tendon from torso,   a language emancipated

into sovereign activity.

As if it waited a century to face what it would always become, the prosthesis is able to, only now, finally come to terms with *us*, the spectator:

as if the cork & oak were a voice ignored as history collapsed forward. It is the confession of a future not yet arrived, yet already here in fullness as this stolen limb.

The leg admits the future is a false branch, one we wear to account for both a past & future we have lived beside but not yet inhabited, a past & future we have occupied but not yet fully acknowledged as sovereign confessions:

> our existing flesh
>
> luminous bruises
>
> touching each other
>
> rackripe & blossomed.

DECLARATION OF INTENTION.

(Invalid for all purposes seven years after the date hereof.)

I, *Chalchiuhtotolin*, aged *before life, as life itself, of all years & fertility*, whose occupation *was the perceiver of truth*, do declare on oath (affirm) that my personal description is: Color *of the wild fowl of the wood & sea*, my complexion *iridescent as hummingbird feathers*, my height, that *of sacrifice, of the rising trees*, my weight: *the burden of godly conduct*; this color of hair: *all the green stone & gold drawn back to the first mother's womb*, the color of my eyes: *marigold twined with feasting & dancing—now, everything seen: smoking mirrors*; other visible distinctive marks *I was the shape of a giant garbed in colored tissue paper but, now, all my fertile powers are but shards*; I was born in *the waters before birth* on the day of *the first liquid* anno Domini _____ ; I now reside *between bondage & deprivation within these varieties of existence*; I emigrated to the United States of America from *the Law of Compensation* on the vessel *of the sinner, they who, at the end of existence, will appear on the throne of the solar gods, elevating them to holiness*; my last foreign residence was *within the four elements evolved into mineral, animal and vegetable, there, I drank from a bird's beak, his gullet full of fermented honey water*.

It is my bona fide intention to renounce forever all allegiance and fidelity to any foreign prince, potentate, state, or sovereignty, and particularly to *Ehecatl, God of the Wind*, of which I am now a citizen (subject); I arrived at the (Port) of *sound*, as *a gift to Shamash, the Sun*, in the State (Territory or District) of *Tonacacuauhtitlan, the place of the Tree of Sustenance* on or about *the first* day of *filial devotion & conjugal regard* anno Domini _____ ; I am not an anarchist; I am not a polygamist nor a believer in the practice of polygamy; and it is my intention in good faith to become a citizen of the United States of America and to permanently reside therein.

So help me God.

(Original signature of declarant) _____ Subscribed and sworn to (affirmed) before me this _____ day of _____, anno Domini _____

[L. 8.]   (Official character of attestor.)

PETITION FOR NATURALIZATION.

_____ Court of _____ .

In the matter of the petition of _____ to be admitted as
a citizen of the United States of America.

To the _____ Court:

The petition of _____ respectfully shows:

First. My full name is _Chalchiuhtotolin_

Second. My place of residence is numbered _outside number on No_ street, city
of _Absence in the Shape of a Fountain_, State (Territory or District) of _Xibalba_

Third. My occupation _was the keeping of the divine fire, a serpent with maiden
eyes_.

Fourth. I was born on the _dissemination_ day of _carnations, stillness wrung black_.

Fifth. I emigrated to the United States from _the elemental letters_, on or about
the _final praising_ day of _the shriven light_, anno Domini _____ ,
and arrived at the port of _the last voices justified among the orchards_ in the United
States, on the vessel _whose light spilled the tempest feast_.

Sixth. I declared my intention to become a citizen of the United States on
the _androgynous_ day of _when all that was "primitive" vanished_ at _the latitude in
my blood_, in the _laws of analogy whose_ court of _broken images erected sanctity
below her shape_.

Seventh. I am _the virgin_ married. My wife's name is _contained in the One,
martyrdom sustaining me_. She was born in _this snow, this cluster of rage spreading
the rose_ and now resides at _end of narrative, salt shaped to summer's fading scents_.
I have, _beneath the noun, buried all my_ children, and the name, date and
place of birth and place of residence of each of said children is as follows
_____ ; _____ ; _____ .

Eighth. I am not a disbeliever in or opposed to organized government or a
member of or affiliated with any organization or body of persons teaching
disbelief in organized government. I am not a polygamist nor a believer in
the practice of polygamy.

I am attached to the principles of the Constitution of the United States, and
it is my intention to become a citizen of the United States and to renounce

absolutely and forever all allegiance and fidelity to any foreign prince, potentate, state, or sovereignty, and particularly to *my body as murmur, that capacity of joy full of flowers in me*, of which at this time I am a citizen (or subject), and it is my intention to reside permanently in the United States.

Ninth. I am able to speak the English language.

[EXECUTIVE ORDER]

The crisis crown. black thorns piercing. for of
inviolate flesh a replica of flesh. dioramas of bodies.
lashed & stretched. trunk opened for reverence. in
the thickening. death of the compound. noun we
are. bones bleached to bear. wings of dried lungs.
paling the sovereign. for the world speech defies.

SKIN MAPS

i.

An MP in Phanrang, my father watched the night grow dense from a tower in Juliet sector. The camp's mortar pits fired flares of dissonant light through the arid fields of barb & weed. The tower's shadows stretched out as starved fingers clawing at the jungle.

The Vietcong's zappers, carrying satchel chargers of c-4, would attempt the base's walls in the obscurity. Crawling figures caught the flare light, subduing it within themselves—bodies a reservoir of uncertainty. Once, one drew near the wall beneath Juliet-5, my father's tower.

He watched the boy approach arm over arm through the camp's drainage ditch. Glare from the flares distinguished the strained movements of breath, lips like a charcoal etch thin above the chin. To frighten the boy away, my father fired rounds around the small figure. Arm over arm, the boy continued.

Today, my father doesn't say how bullets barraged the boy's body, skipped mud up where missed; my father doesn't say the blood splashed like murky water from beneath a skipping stone; nor does he say how, after, the boy lay beneath wire & weed, motionless in the mortar light, hair billowing like black wheat.

He says, "The Orange sifted from a thrumming plane." The fine particles of white powder burrowing inward until his skin lost tint in patterned locations across his body, leaving him chalk-white markings—skin a war map of erasure. He tells me, rubbing his arms as if cleansing them, he just wants to forget.

ii.

At birth, I was diagnosed with a form of porphyria cutanea tarda, a skin defect where the skin may thin & blister in sun-exposed areas (common to offspring of those exposed to the pesticide known as Agent Orange).

As my mother remembers, she once took me to the shade of a maple. After a year beneath the soft white of lamps, doctors felt it safe to reveal me unblemished to the sun. I was dressed in Sunday suit: blue vest, pants, black tie. Stroller rolling beside, my parents walked me to the neighborhood playground. Our Caucasian neighbors asked my mother— when had my family adopted a white child? At the park, a warm wind tickled the leaves into clucking tongues. My mother watched my father play baseball, blankets sheltered me in the stroller from the sun. After a time, she glimpsed through the covering, gasped: my fingers, face were traced in veins, blistering from the warm spring breeze. Later that day, when she saw my sunburned white, my tia coyly quipped—"Whose honky baby is that?"

iii.

As nails from the skin, you feel skin

nailed to the body. At birth,

little hammers made the skin

stay. Now, the nails want

out: the blood for the cauliflower

cloud. You want to be clean. You

needle the purple, purple the eye

under the eye. You needle

your white head, your black head

     from the pore you
     scrub you wash your
     skin tender like small

     feathers you want to be
     clean you want

     the skin as silk as your skin
     punctures to thorns

like guillotines like
small feathers tender

like fathers you tie
a noose on the garage concrete

you cry a funeral you

would want hydrangea orchids
a wicker bird cage

       with butterflies   your mother
       crying butterflies your body
       like wax clean   flowers cut
       from the body
       you want
       the one purple below

       your eye to disappear
       a black thorn closing

       the tear duct eyes swelled
       black swelled shut you would
       want a black
       tie suit
       crying your body a cage
       of wax you would write

       to love is conceiving you
       as abandonment. Reborn.

One story has been an invitation,
the other:

has been only a frame to splice the windless expectations of discretion

has been a sky punctured into magnolia

has been filled with women drowned in flags

has been the incarnation radiant with the forsythia's undivided suffering

has been his heaven whose history is the body

IV

CHAS. EISENMANN. PORTRAITS TAKEN INSTANTANEOUSLY. 229 BOWERY, N. Y.

Is there a relation, a sensible harmony between moral and physical beauty? Between moral turpitude and corporal deformity? Or, is there a real disagreement between moral beauty and physical deformity, between moral deformity and corporal beauty?

—JOHANN CASPAR LAVATER,
*Essays on Physiognomy: Designed to Promote Knowledge
and the Love of Mankind,* 1789

THE RED ANCHOR

> his lip's
> grace grails
> the bullet
> for lung
> to breathe
> music turned
> sharper bell

His chest opened in wreaths of polished bone. A red anchor lowered from the puncture & winter's field built its white altar beneath our hands. Now, I sprinkle glass where we buried the threshing house, my mouth & tongue a flower of ambulance sirens.

[ ]

> Articulation became instinct
> thinned to shadow
> of light not body
> eye muted
> into vows
> the seasons unfurled
> with distance woven
> with beginning touch

On the gurney, he became a series of questions. Life exigent with carnations.

I said, "

."

[ ]

A straw body
limping
he lay
an eye dried
in memory's
measureless
violence   if the body
were a self
his would coin

After I wept, my hands shot the confession crossing the wire. I saw black thorns in the animal we are. I didn't hear.

I didn't.

OF MAXIMO AND BARTOLA, THE AZTEC CHILDREN

Exhibited in "The Gallery of Wonders" of P. T. Barnum's American Museum in the 1850s, Maximo & Bartola were promoted as "Aztec Wonders." The children were, in actuality, of unknown national origin; some speculate they were from El Salvador or Nicaragua. In addition to a cognitive disability, the children possessed small statures & elongated skulls. Based upon these characteristics, they were classified "as living specimens of an antique race nearly extinct" in the forty-eight-page pamphlet published for their exhibition. Lavishly entitled,

> *Illustrated Memoir of an Eventful Expedition into Central America Resulting in the Discovery of the Idolatrous City of Iximaya, in an Unexplored Region; and the possession of two remarkable Aztec Children, Maximo (the boy), and Bartola (the girl), Descendants and Specimens of the Sacerdotal Caste (now nearly extinct), of the Ancient Aztec Founders of the Ruined Temples of that Country,*

the purported memoir sketched a garish account of an expedition into Latin America where one "Pedro Velasquez" came into possession of the children. Appropriating an appellation out of a cheap romance novel, the pamphlet's author was, in fact, the "explorer" John Lloyd Stephens.

Stephens's gratuitous travel narratives had established him, in the popular imagination of the mid-19th century, as having "discovered" the "lost" Mayan culture. Stephens's adopting that moniker, "Pedro Velasquez," to authenticate his fiction linguistically mirrors & extends the imperial appropriation & human trafficking of Maximo & Bartola. A species of authorial conceptual minstrelsy

> upon children unbodied
> as many mansions
> of caesura in negative theology.

The "Aztecs" *did* practice body modification for rituals, particularly,
cranial modification for the royal class:

> deforming the pliable
>
> cranial bones of an infant:
>
> her skull assured
> & pressed
>
> between padded planks, stretching
> the head shape—ruined temples
>
> most humanly dedicated

Today, Maximo & Bartola are understood as having suffered microcephaly. In the 19th century, they were rendered "ethnological curiosities." As the fictitious "true account" styles, in the jungles of South America the children were revered as sacred ciphers of an incarnate mythology. Staring, their bodies perversely render ethnic heritage a sideshow curiosity as well as a sadomasochistic playhouse of appropriations deserving of worship.

The ethnopolitical subject, an appropriation of an evidence in time, an emblem cascading through fact.

> To an ancient anecdotal caste
>
>> of the Sacerdotal Class
>> turbans decorated with three
>> large plumes of the squezal,
>
> coronals of gay feathers   arranged within a blue cloth,
>
>> the cardinal points of the horizon:
>
>> an ear was applied there
>> to receive an unexpected world.

Displayed worldwide, from Buckingham Palace

> to New York,
> the brother & sister
> became testaments of a sacred analogy
>
> between mercantile speculation & the silence of history.

As the years progressed, their fame diminished, as did their "guardian's" revenue. As a publicity stunt, Maximo & Bartola were "married." Advertisers defended the nuptials by touting that the "Aztec practice" of incest warranted & sanctioned the ceremony. Pimped for the perversity of white desire, Maximo & Bartola performed the profane. Photographs of the occasion were sold.

The "they" unnamed.

She wore a satin wedding dress & he was

a silhouette devoured by sand

dressed in fine black evening

wear. Fist held at his waist,

Maximo balanced himself

against her chair; a pearl necklace ringed her neck,

a corsage spilling

out of his breast pocket

into empty shells

the Lilliputian wonders,

   to which these children
   are assumed to pertain

   —still, bright lakes of water
   glowed among them—

whatever their origin
      & ascent, they are here:
      in the silence of history,

      in their sculptural costume,
      vines covered with flowers,

      the folding gates
      in their fullest perfection

      & less than a human face

To speak from the evidence of his own eyesight,
fragmentary throughout,

        the difference is so distinctive, indeed, from the Caucasian,
        the Mongolian, the African, & Red American races, that the
        mere glance is sufficient to carry conviction of their separate

individuality as a race

more strange than the vast skeletons of the Mastodon

        but like the black swan

        fallen under observation

	Boy. (Maximo) 17 years of age		GIRL (Bartola) 11 years	
	inches	lines	inches	lines
height from sole to vertex	34	6	30	9
Length of Spinal Column	16	0	15	8
Arm (Humerus)	7	0	6	6
Ulna	5	9	5	3
Hand	4	0	4	2
Breadth of Hand	2	3	2	0

The great Toe is well developed and the Foot other well formed in both.

	Weight 23lbs		21½lbs	
Circumference of Cranium (Head)	13	3	13	4
Antero-posterior diameter	4	3	4	6

From one Meatus Auditorius to the other
        around the forehead
        Ditto   over the Vertex
        Ditto   around the Occiput
From root of nose over Head to the
        occipital-spine

living specimens of an antique race nearly extinct

> *reticulated buskins*
> *of red cord, black hair,*
> *tastefully disposed;*

> *the first migration of these people—*
> *all that was visible*
> *as the living city*

> *that first enshrined them,*
> *dense clouds rising*
> *upon the natural sequence of the narrative*

the true gospel

parrots & spiritual existences
glide in & out
upon every hand

the phoenix of the vegetable world   blooms, once, & perishes

at the palace
shot through the body,

from every stem,

a history of a hundred hymned summers
birds unending.

BROWN I SEE YOU, BROWN I DON'T
The Other-Race Effect (ORE)

I'm shaping ground beef into the round of a burger patty when I feel a tap on the shoulder.

"You're Mexican?" His pockmarked face scars into a scowl.
"Yep."
"You're white, bro. You don't speak Spanish?"
"Naw."
"Me neither."

I had worked with him for over two weeks in the greasy confines of the kitchen. I knew we were the only Latinos working here. When I had tried to speak to him before he would simply point me to someone else.

A white waitress, eavesdropping, shouts, "You didn't know he was Mexican! Look at those cheekbones and skin, he can't be white!"

The ORE was initially named after C. A. Feingold's studies of an environment's influence on perception. Feingold may have given birth to a cliché when his 1914 study proposed, "people are not that good at individualizing faces belonging to another racial group and may find that faces from other races *all look alike*." While it may be easy to dismiss a statement like this made in 1914, what can't be disregarded is, sadly, the weight of scientific evidence supporting Feingold's statement. Studies on race identification, like Feingold's, have a long history; however, this has only recently been enriched by face perception studies in neurophysiology.

According to the 2011 *Oxford Handbook of Face Perception*, "Face perception is a high-level process . . . result[ing] from the interaction of the incoming information and internal representations." Facial recognition is a composite of both the socio-environmental context in which the perception occurs and one's experiential knowledge. Other researchers, A. G. Goldstein and R. L. Gregory, assert, "Early and extensive exposure to a set of visual stimuli" constructs "a schema." This schema results from, and is continually modified by, experience. If one has experience with people of color, the studies demonstrate, one has a better chance of *perceiving* each body for its individualizing characteristics and will *not* defer to rendering a perceived body according to a particular pre-fashioned generalized "schema."

"You smoke weed?" he asks.

He looks like my brother Mark, hard edged and quiet, face volcanic. He gestures for me to follow. He unties his apron and throws it on top of a box of avocados.

Outside, we both lean against a dumpster. As he rolls the joint, his intensity is the same as a boy in a confessional. We pass it between us, inhaling the smoke deep, exhaling the differences.

Stoned, eyes like crimson rosary beads, he looks through me, makes me feel as transparent as broken glass.

The precision in the studies performed over the past thirty years is almost laughable: contemporary studies analyze racial recognition occurring in the recognizing or "perceiving" of the "eye-brow distance in Eastern Asian faces" or when racial recognition activates in the cortical region of the brain "between 60 and 90 degrees of angle of face rotation." Analyzing the minutest details, these reports find, "in most societies, people's visual experience during development is limited to faces that share a certain morphology, i.e. faces of a certain racial group." Neurophysiologists Bruno Rossion and Caroline Michel assert, with increasing experience, these shared morphologies eventually generate a "holistic representation."

Citing studies of children from 2004 to 2009, the *Oxford Handbook of Face Perception* asserts children as young as seven months exhibit this kind of "holistic mode of processing." Rossion and Michel, building on such work, find these holistic representations, as a person gains more experience, "originally *broadly tuned*, become more fine-grained, or *finely tuned* for a certain racial group of faces." The studies in neurology describe how perception is "auto-tuned."

That night, I walk through deep snow.
My boots punch holes into the eggshell
surface, slowly working toward a path.
The houses in the distance hold the
night around them like discarded black
holes. Stepping on the concrete path,
I kick off the white chunks sticking to
my corduroy pants.

Down the street, a house is lit with
frost. I see a group of boys, some
putting up a flag, others huddling
around a grill. I cross the street
opposite them as I approach.

"Spic, hey, spic, we got a burrito
cooking over here," a voice calls.

"Come on over, wetback, you can eat
and we won't call la migra or nothing
until after you're done."

One frat boy steps forward, dressed in
a suit, flutters a stream of Spanish at me.
"Espero que ustedes puedan venir."

The words hum from his mouth like
dragonflies, wings glittering in the
light. I see them rise to chase stars.

In neurology, with time and "tuning,"
the ability to recognize a person of a
shared racial schema is broadened to
include a diverse range of data, allowing
for *perception* and *recognition* of differences
in alignment of facial features, color
hair, clothing, etc. Broadly stated, the
continued perceptual experiencing of
racial difference allows for more difference
to be perceived and, consequently, be
recognized as a difference within one's
own constituency. To emphasize, to even
be perceived, difference must be learned.
In contrast, faces whose characteristics *do
not* harmonize with that shared racialized
schema are "analyzed feature-by-feature";
in other words, the racial other's face is
processed *in pieces*. The Other-Race Effect
(ORE) results from this piecemeal manner
of perceptual processing.

The frat boy flutters another flock of language. "No habla espanol? Esta muy pobrecito."

His tongue is soft cotton candy pink, glistening.

My mind races: I want his tongue. To slice it, cut it out as if I were circumcising. I want to circumcise his tongue, remove it like foreskin. Foreskin. Before skin. Before flesh. Before flesh there was the word and the word was God. I want to cut out his tongue and swallow the foreskin of God.

"Wetback, what the fuck are you smiling at?"

I realize I'm leaning against a tree, glaring at them.

They start walking toward me. Dodging into the night, my skin fades snow-blind into the gray.

Rossion and Michel assert ORE occurs because "these faces are not or [are] processed less holistically." Forgiving Rossion and Michel's awkward phrasing, they are saying the racial other's particular face, when perceived, *is either "processed" partially or not at all* AT THE VERY MOMENT OF CORTICAL PROCESSING. One might say, when racialized others are seen by the uninitiated, they are perceived in pieces and, likely, understood only as caricatures.

For Rossion and Michel, the ORE acts as a kind of strategy of perception by which those of a same race (SR) are perceived *as individuals* and *as part of an in-group* collective; however, an individual of another race "cannot fit well with the holistic template because its morphology is beyond the range of morphologies generally encountered in the perceiver's environment." Other races, according to the *Oxford Handbook*, are not immediately perceived as *individuals*; rather, the perceiver falls back on their context's particular generalized schema (caricature) for dealing with that particular racial group.

THE CURANDERA'S TALE OF THE AGAVE'S BLOOM

Dust settled in his peppered beard as he wandered into the desert to die. His eldest son was dead by the hand of his youngest. His wife *Maria Jesus* & his daughter of the same name had fled. An agave's white blossom curved in the wind. More dust settled. He stumbled. Olive eyes swallowed the sky. The tears soaked into the cracks of his blotched skin, muddied rivulets ran through his thick beard. He fell to his knees. Sand settled deeply into the pockets of his hands. A blossom curved.

Later, the old General found Don Beltran's body: he gently touched the blistered forehead, loosed the two fists of sand from his friend's grip, & poured them into a leather satchel. He had killed the man's youngest son himself: his arthritic grip drove knifepoint past the thin ribs into the heart. He'd made himself stare into the boy's startled, watering eyes. He had been his *Nino*, his godfather; he remembered helping the boy spell his name with charcoal on vellum, those eyes just as wide then, just as watery. He left the Don's body to the desert & took the worn leather satchel to his ranch in the fields of north Guanajuato. He siphoned the sand into two spiraled snail shells. Positioning them on a mantel beneath a portrait of his father, he caressed their whorl & curve.

One hundred & fifty years after the old General's death, the shelled sand sought the Don's great-great-granddaughter *Maria Jesus Beltran*. She received the brown spotted shells under auspicious circumstances: a curandero bought them from a dealer of wasp wings & salty chapulines. Trusting this man who had delivered her firstborn, Maria Jesus carried the shells on raised palms like communion wafers. Pregnant, she followed the curandero's instructions & planted the crustaceans in her youngest son's name; a year later, an agave's white bloom emerged from his first spoken word. Plucking the bloom, Maria Jesus made a tea from its white. She took the tea, poured it over the heads of her sons, baptizing them. Beneath each child's forehead, the thousand pages of their destinies grew wet, ink smearing. The children wept black tears. Collecting her children's grievings in a jar, Maria Jesus wrapped the glass with rosaries & placed it beneath a portrait of her mother.

One day each year, this jar's water blooms with rotted agave petals. On this day the Beltran women with the name *Maria Jesus* gather. In a circle, they feed a single tar-swollen petal to each male in their family. These children, in time, are bestowed the betrayals intended for their family: disease, love's misfortune & untimely death fall into their soft hands. The eldest daughter inherits the rosary-wrapped jar & the portrait. In contrition, this daughter dutifully collects her life's tears in the jar. Salted barren beneath the task of her name, her womb blackens. On her funeral day, beneath a chorus of olive eyes, an unnamed infant is placed in her opened coffin. Laid on the body's shrouded breast, the babe's fist is inserted into the corpse's rouged mouth. The Beltrans wait for the small hand to emerge wet with an agave's white blossom.

THE WAKE OF MARIA DE JESUS MARTINEZ

Disbudded chrysanthemum
florets ring her casket:

    oak laid,
    my grandmother's arms

cross; gilded gold,
her bold button'd suit

lies black against white satin;
oak grieved, her daughter kneels

tear-pearled & sorrow sung:

tear-pearled & sorrow sung:

the furnaces hunger

within my mother's cry,

love mother'd what love must hate—

the gasping erasure

be   her   *fore her*

cut *be/fore* away:

be/fore away:
Maria Jesus

grin sly beneath her
waist-long silver
hair, cigarette thin

in her slender
hand, she glances

outside the frame
into image's inevitable

collapse; or, with what paper-soft

collapse; or, with what paper-soft

        steeple'd hands,
        she leads

        me to dream in
        fatherlessness:

        some men wear
        every organ a throne:

I wear my grandmother's hearse,

        a shell gasping black
        burdened by body.

        I mean to say I am
        hiding, I mean I am holding

her rosary: as pale oval as

her rosary: as pale oval as

                peppermint candies

                half-sucked
                        &
                sugar sweet

                bone-blanched,
                slick with

                the extended definition
                of some distant

steeple'd faith:
                as pale oval as

steeple'd faith:

as pale oval as

death
bound her hands
a rose-nest
of mood & form
unbridled

from within.

unbridled

from within.

a ceaseless cancer
ate her silence

&, now,

four mourner rows stand
before my fugitive eyes:

&

I agree
to conduct

I agree
to conduct

her a dollhouse

sermon of plastic–pink
comfort flowers.

Comfort flowers
    a sermon of
    plastic comfort pinking.

& I said,

Death matron'd my mother

    of her mother matron:

    a three year
    slice of

    night falling
    & what patient

    blackrot shook
    her lung black.

Her lung black,

I said, I know why the lamb white
wooed the lion:

to uplift the last
of all letters,

all the ardor pure.
God-make,

make god my
unconscious soon born

sober sunburn.
Soon, you cry, I

too soon cry,
soon—to—soon

each other's soon, sung
for each's soon.

For each's soon, I said,
    my mother knelt
        & cried, I said,

    There is only the fall:
        like leaves grasping,
        we are each's first sketch.

    The shoots bud upon the branch
        & I say, I think we are loved.

        & I know we are loved.

For each's soon, I said,
You held for each's soon.

WHERE LOVE IS GROUND TO WHEAT

for Maria Jesus Martinez

You were laid among lilies,

        the thin skin of
        the leaf, the interval, oak

            pews bowing beneath the weight.

If a stone were cast, your mouth
would be the well anchoring the water's

wish. And the word you would speak
in that incommensurable depth

            could unlock space with a paper key.

            Beside the casket, I collect my tears
            before they fall so I may look at you,

so the white down of children may fill the empty beaches again,
so the bees may store the honey

            where mercy prepares the map
            of the forgiven within us.

                We are too many skies,
                we who cling to the visible,

& the bread of my routines,

                now absent of you,
                are abundant with you.

ACKNOWLEDGMENTS

The author is deeply grateful to the editors of *Misrepresented People* from NYQ Books, the *Denver Quarterly, Visible Binary,* and *PoetryNow* from the Poetry Foundation for featuring earlier versions of these poems.

Great thanks to my friends and family for their support during these years of difficult decisions: Jeffrey Pethybridge, Carolina Ebeid, & Patrick Pethybridge—endless friendship & gratitude; Andrea Rexilius & Eric Baus—I don't know where/who I'd be without you; Rosebud Ben-Oni, Khadijah Queen, Mathias Svalina, Chris Rosales, Juliette Lee, Joshua Ware, Julie Carr, Vincent Toro & Grisel Acosta, Matthew Thomas, Joshua Stacey, Peggy Yocom, Jennifer Atkinson, Eric Pankey, Susan Tichy, Jerry & Mary Martinez, Mark Martinez, Ivan Martinez, Tiffany Martinez, Dante Martinez, Talia Martinez, Tyler Martinez, Trinity Martinez.

Carmen Giménez Smith—My friend & mentor, editor & punk rock superstar, thank you & I love you.

Teresa Rosa Veramendi—You, my light ever swiftly.

NOTES

TREATY OF GUADALUPE HIDALGO

Language collected and collaged from Richard Griswold del Castillo's translation of the treaty as found in his book *The Treaty of Guadalupe Hidalgo: A Legacy of Conflict* (Norman: University of Oklahoma Press, 1990).

CASTA PAINTINGS, AN EROTICS OF NEGATION

Farid Matuk, *This Isa Nice Neighborhood* (Tucson, AZ: Letter Machine Editions, 2010), p. 9.

Casta images, Spanish names and translations from Ilona Katzew, *Casta Painting: Images of Race in Eighteenth-Century Mexico* (New Haven, CT: Yale University Press, 2004). Her book also offers detailed accounts of particular & general legislative cases involving the use of castas in the court.

THE HEAD OF JOAQUIN MURRIETA

Los Angeles Star (September 3, 1853), p. 2.

MUSEUM OF THE AMERICAS

Christopher Taylor, "The Limbs of Empire," *American Literature* 83, no. 1 (2011).

Herman Melville, in *American Geographics: U.S. National Narratives and the Representation of the Non-European World, 1830–1865*, ed. Bruce Harvey (Stanford, CA: Stanford University Press, 2001).

Bill Hatcher, "Captured Leg of Santa Anna," RoadsideAmerica.com, http://www.roadsideamerica.com/story/18808. Accessed May, 2011.

THESE LANDS ARE OUTLINED IN ARTICLE V OF THE TREATY.

Richard Griswold del Castillo, *The Treaty of Guadalupe Hidalgo*, p. 86.

Martha Menchaca, *Recovering History, Constructing Race: The Indian, Black, and White Roots of Mexican Americans* (Austin: University of Texas Press, 2001), p. 218.

Maurice Merleau-Ponty, *The Visible and the Invisible*, ed. Claude Lefort, trans. Alphonso Lingis (Chicago: Northwestern University Press, 1968), p. 132;

"because each of the two beings is an archetype for the other,
because the body belongs to the order of the things as the world is
universal flesh," p. 137.

OF MAXIMO AND BARTOLA, THE AZTEC CHILDREN

All italicized language has been collaged from John L. Stephens, *Illustrated Memoir of an Eventful Expedition into Central America Resulting in the Discovery of the Idolatrous City of Iximaya, in an Unexplored Region; and the possession of two remarkable Aztec Children, Maximo (the boy), and Bartola (the girl), Descendants and Specimens of the Sacerdotal Caste (now nearly extinct), of the Ancient Aztec Founders of the Ruined Temples of that Country* (New York: Wynkoop, Hallenbeck & Thomas Printers, 1860). Print.

MARIA JESUS MARTINEZ, 2013

JOHN ASHBERY
Selected Poems
Self-Portrait in a Convex
    Mirror

PAUL BEATTY
Joker, Joker, Deuce

JOSHUA BENNETT
The Sobbing School

TED BERRIGAN
The Sonnets

LAUREN BERRY
The Lifting Dress

PHILIP BOOTH
Lifelines: Selected Poems
    1950–1999

JULIANNE BUCHSBAUM
The Apothecary's Heir

JIM CARROLL
Fear of Dreaming: The
    Selected Poems
Living at the Movies
Void of Course

ALISON HAWTHORNE DEMING
Genius Loci
Rope
Stairway to Heaven

CARL DENNIS
Another Reason
Callings
New and Selected Poems
    1974–2004
Night School
Practical Gods
Ranking the Wishes
Unknown Friends

DIANE DI PRIMA
Loba

STUART DISCHELL
Dig Safe

STEPHEN DOBYNS
Velocities: New and
    Selected Poems:
    1966–1992

EDWARD DORN
Way More West

ROGER FANNING
The Middle Ages

ADAM FOULDS
The Broken Word

CARRIE FOUNTAIN
Burn Lake
Instant Winner

AMY GERSTLER
Crown of Weeds
Dearest Creature
Ghost Girl
Medicine
Nerve Storm
Scattered at Sea

EUGENE GLORIA
Drivers at the Short-Time
    Motel
Hoodlum Birds
My Favorite Warlord

DEBORA GREGER
By Herself
Desert Fathers, Uranium
    Daughters
God
In Darwin's Room
Men, Women, and Ghosts
Western Art

TERRANCE HAYES
American Sonnets for
    My Past and Future
    Assassin
Hip Logic
How to Be Drawn
Lighthead
Wind in a Box

NATHAN HOKS
The Narrow Circle

ROBERT HUNTER
Sentinel and Other Poems

MARY KARR
Viper Rum

JACK KEROUAC
Book of Blues
Book of Haikus
Book of Sketches

JOANNA KLINK
Circadian
Excerpts from a Secret
    Prophecy
Raptus

JOANNE KYGER
As Ever: Selected Poems

ANN LAUTERBACH
Hum
If in Time: Selected Poems,
    1975–2000
On a Stair
Or to Begin Again
Spell
Under the Sign

CORINNE LEE
Plenty

PHILLIS LEVIN
May Day
Mercury
Mr. Memory & Other
    Poems

PATRICIA LOCKWOOD
Motherland Fatherland
    Homelandsexuals

WILLIAM LOGAN
Macbeth in Venice
Madame X
Rift of Light
Strange Flesh
The Whispering Gallery

J. MICHAEL MARTINEZ
Museum of the Americas

ADRIAN MATEJKA
The Big Smoke
Map to the Stars
Mixology

MICHAEL MCCLURE
Huge Dreams: San
    Francisco and Beat
    Poems

ROSE MCLARNEY
Its Day Being Gone

DAVID MELTZER
David's Copy: The Selected
    Poems of David Meltzer

ROBERT MORGAN
Dark Energy
Terroir

CAROL MUSKE-DUKES
Blue Rose
An Octave Above Thunder
Red Trousseau
Twin Cities

ALICE NOTLEY
Certain Magical Acts
Culture of One
The Descent of Alette
Disobedience
In the Pines
Mysteries of Small Houses

WILLIE PERDOMO
The Essential Hits of
    Shorty Bon Bon

LIA PURPURA
It Shouldn't Have Been
    Beautiful

LAWRENCE RAAB
The History of Forgetting
Visible Signs: New and
    Selected Poems

BARBARA RAS
The Last Skin
One Hidden Stuff

MICHAEL ROBBINS
Alien vs. Predator
The Second Sex

PATTIANN ROGERS
Generations
Holy Heathen Rhapsody
Quickening Fields
Wayfare

SAM SAX
Madness

ROBYN SCHIFF
A Woman of Property

WILLIAM STOBB
Absentia
Nervous Systems

TRYFON TOLIDES
An Almost Pure Empty
    Walking

SARAH VAP
Viability

ANNE WALDMAN
Gossamurmur
Kill or Cure
Manatee/Humanity
Structure of the World
    Compared to a Bubble
Trickster Feminism

JAMES WELCH
Riding the Earthboy 40

PHILIP WHALEN
Overtime: Selected Poems

ROBERT WRIGLEY
Anatomy of Melancholy
    and Other Poems
Beautiful Country
Box
Earthly Meditations: New
    and Selected Poems
Lives of the Animals
Reign of Snakes

MARK YAKICH
The Importance of Peeling
    Potatoes in Ukraine
Unrelated Individuals
    Forming a Group
    Waiting to Cross